D0529330

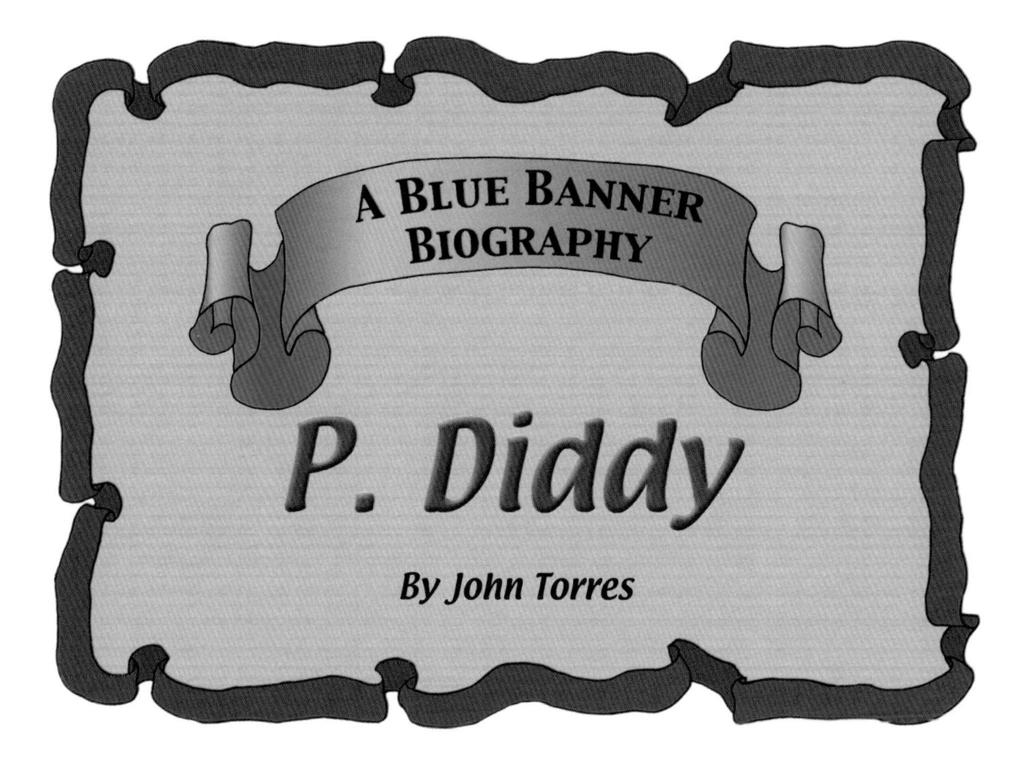

P.O. Box 196
Hockessin, Delaware 19707
Visit us on the web: www.mitchelllane.com
Comments? email us: mitchelllane@mitchelllane.com

Printing 2 3 4 5 6 7 8 9

Blue Banner Biographies

Alicia Keys
Ashlee Simpson
Beyoncé
Christina Aguilera
Condoleezza Rice
Eminem
Jay-Z
Jodie Foster
Lance Armstrong
Mary-Kate and Ashley Olsen
Missy Elliott
Paris Hilton
Rita Williams-Garcia
Sally Field
Usher
Allen Iverson
Ashton Kutcher
Bow Wow
Christopher Paul Curtis
Daniel Radcliffe
Eve
Jennifer Lopez
Justin Berfield
Lindsay Lohan
Melissa Gilbert
Nelly
Queen Latifah
Ron Howard
Selena
Ashanti
Avril Lavigne
Britney Spears
Clay Aiken
Derek Jeter
Ja Rule
J.K. Rowling
Kate Hudson
Mario
Michael Jackson
P. Diddy
Ritchie Valens
Rudy Giuliani
Shirley Temple

Library of Congress Cataloging-in-Publication Data
Torres, John Albert.
P. Diddy / John Torres.
p. cm — (Blue banner biography)
Includes bibliographical references and index.
Discography: p.
ISBN 1-58415-315-6 (library bound)
1. P. Diddy, 1970—Juvenile literature. 2. Rap musicians—United States—Biography—Juvenile literature. I. Title. II. Series.
ML3930.P84T67 2004
782.421649'092—dc22

2004021881

ABOUT THE AUTHOR: John A. Torres is an award-winning journalist covering social issues for *Florida Today Newspaper*. John has also written more than 25 books for various publishers on a variety of topics. He wrote *Marc Anthony*, *Mia Hamm*, and *Fitness Stars of Bodybuilding* for Mitchell Lane Publishers. In his spare time John likes playing sports, going to theme parks, and fishing with his children, step-children, and wife, Jennifer.

PHOTO CREDITS: Cover, p. 4—Brad Barket/Getty Images; p. 9—Frank Micelotta/Getty Images; p. 17—Thos Robinson/Getty Images; p. 21—Frank Micelotta/Getty Images; p. 23—Eric Ryan/Getty Images; p. 26—Paul Hawthorne/Getty Images; p. 28—Frank Micelotta/Getty Images.
ACKNOWLEDGMENTS: The following story has been thoroughly researched, and to the best of our knowledge, represents a true story. While every possible effort has been made to ensure accuracy, the publisher will not assume liability for damages caused by inaccuracies in the data, and makes no warranty on the accuracy of the information contained herein. This story has not been authorized nor endorsed by P. Diddy.

CONTENTS

As a producer, performer, and actor P. Diddy is an all-around entertainment legend.

New York, New York

The audience is silent. Their attention is riveted. They are waiting for Sean Combs, also known as music superstar P. Diddy, to speak.

Finally, he does. Only, it's not P. Diddy. Combs has transformed himself into Walter Lee Younger.

"Willy! Willy . . . don't do it. . . . Man, not with that money!" he exclaims in an anguished, high-pitched voice. "Man . . . That money is made out of my father's flesh."

The audience rises to their feet at the end of this climactic scene in the Broadway play *A Raisin in the Sun*. And once again, P. Diddy has proven just about everyone wrong.

When he was signed to play the starring role in the 2004 version of the 1960 play, most critics thought it was a prank to sell tickets. But the play became a Broadway success. Written by renowned African American playwright Lorraine Hansberry, it tells the story of a poor black family's struggles with dreams and racial prejudice after coming into a load of money. And though Combs did not win any individual honors, his acting helped actress Phylicia Rashad, who played his mother, win a Tony Award. A good actor is capable of making the other actors on stage better, and that's just what Combs did.

A good actor is capable of making the other actors on stage better, and that's what Combs did.

In fact, Rashad became the first black actress to ever win the Tony Award—Broadway's highest honor—for a dramatic role.

While his performance did surprise some, it wasn't Combs's first attempt at acting. In 2001 he appeared in the film *Made,* and he appeared opposite Oscar-winner Halle Berry in *Monster's Ball.*

Combs was not ready to stop there. The rap superstar and award-winning clothing designer hopes to become the next big movie star.

"I think I'm ready to take that leap," he said. "I'm one to watch in Hollywood. I'm not tooting my own horn, but I definitely feel that I have something that I can bring to the table. As an actor, I'd like to get out there and hone my craft."

Combs credits his New York City background for the fact that he has been successful at just about everything he has done.

"I'm a definite stereotypical New Yorker. I love everything about New York," he said. "I kind of represent that drive and determination in the sense of the lyric, 'If you can make it here, you can make it anywhere.' Being a New Yorker, you have a certain type of heart and drive and way of life. We work hard and we play hard."

Combs credits his New York City background for the fact that he has been successful at just about everything he has done.

But these days, even when Combs plays hard, there seems to be some sort of drive or purpose.

In fact, he hosted a July Fourth party on Long Island, New York, in which he showed up with an original copy of the Declaration of Independence. He flew the cast of *A Raisin in the Sun* on two chartered helicopters to the party, which was part party and part political rally for one of Combs's newest ventures.

He started an organization known as Citizen Change, an effort to get minorities and younger people out to polling places to vote.

"Citizen Change is going to hip young people and minorities to the game," he said. "I don't really have faith in politicians or politics but I have faith in the power of the people, and if we educate ourselves about the hustle, we can make things right."

Combs traveled around the country months before the 2004 presidential election in order to try to get people out to vote.

The organization's emphasis is on education, health care, and jobs, but remains nonpartisan. That means that Combs is avoiding trying to tell people who to vote for. He just wants people to educate themselves, learn about the candidates, and vote.

Combs traveled around the country months before the 2004 presidential election in order to try to get people out to vote.

"There are only a few people in America who have the energy and enthusiasm to get young people to step up to the plate and get excited and passionate about this election, and I'm one of them," he said.

This passion, both on the stage and for social change, is a big change and marks a milestone in Sean Combs's maturity and development. After all, he has certainly come a long way from the brash young rapper who burst on the scene in the mid-1990s.

P. Diddy stands alongside fellow rapper, Mase. Getting young people and minorities to come out and vote is a passion for P. Diddy.

Humble Beginnings

Most rap superstars and hip-hop artists claim to have backgrounds and roots in the most dangerous neighborhoods in America. Sean "P. Diddy" Combs not only claims it, he actually lived it.

Combs was born on November 4, 1969, in Harlem, New York. Harlem is one of New York City's oldest and most notorious neighborhoods. It is known as much for its black culture and ethnic foods as for its rampant drug use and high crime statistics.

As an infant, Combs had no idea how close to that world he really was. His father worked for the board of education and as a cab driver. His mother, a beautiful lady, was a model. People in the neighborhood said the two made a lovely couple.

It was obvious right from the start that Sean would likely follow in his mother's footsteps and enjoy the limelight of the stage. When he was only two years old, his mother included him in a fashion show at a local day care center. He stole the show. Everyone oohed and aahed over the little boy.

"As soon as the spotlight hit me, I just embraced it," Combs laughs.

Sean's mother, Janice, was determined to give her children a better life, one that was safe from drugs and crime.

But the good times and the laughter would soon come to a thunderous halt. Even though Combs's father, Melvin, worked two jobs, he certainly could not have been making enough money to buy the family's elaborate furniture and their expensive car: a Mercedes Benz, the fanciest car in their neighborhood.

No, Melvin Combs had started dealing drugs, thinking that was the way to get his family out of poverty. Instead it brought them misery.

Shortly after Sean's sister, Keisha, was born, Melvin left the house to meet some people on a business deal. It went badly, and Melvin was shot and killed.

Sean's mother, Janice, was determined to give her children a better life, one that was safe from drugs and crime. Together, Sean's mother and grandmother, Jessie, worked numerous jobs, but they made sure that one of them was always available to watch the children.

"My mom and grandmom pulled together and kept me off the streets," Combs said.

"My Mom and grandmom pulled together and kept me off the streets," Combs said. Janice became a true-life hero.

Janice became a true-life hero. She became father as well as mother to him. She worked as an assistant teacher, a school bus driver, and an attendant for handicapped children, and she continued modeling. She also knew how ambitious her son was from a very young age. He talked of becoming rich and famous. She always had a standard response.

"Go to school and pay close attention to your teachers if you want to be a millionaire," she would tell him.

Jessie also provided a loving yet disciplined household where Sean and his sister could flourish.

Janice enrolled Sean in something called the Fresh Air Fund—a charity to help inner-city kids. Sean would go away every summer to the country and see how other types of people live. One summer he went to Pennsylvania and spent time among the Amish people, who live without modern conveniences.

But his mother also taught him the toughness that he would need to survive in the world and especially in Harlem. One day, one of the neighborhood children had punched Sean and taken away his skateboard. He ran home to his mother in tears. She told him not to come in until he had retrieved the skateboard. That was a lesson in tough love, and Sean learned to keep what belonged to him and to respect other people's property.

It was during this time, just before Janice would move her family away from the drug-riddled streets of Harlem, that Combs discovered this wonderful new sound on the radio called rap music. He was able to relate to it. It was written and sung by people who looked like him and who came from places like Harlem. It was his music.

> ***It was during this time, just before Janice would move her family away from . . . Harlem, that Combs discovered . . . rap music.***

He started hanging out with a group of kids that called themselves the 7-UP Crew. The one thing they all had in common was that they loved rap music.

It was a sound, a music, that would change his life.

Slave to the Sound

In 1982, Janice gave her children the best gift she could possibly give at that time. She moved the family from the rough streets of Harlem to a place called Mount Vernon, a New York City suburb in Westchester County. There were parks and woods and trees there, and a mix of people that Sean had to learn to relate to and get along with. Moving from Harlem would make Sean a more rounded person and keep him safer.

During this time, Sean began listening to rap and hip-hop sounds from groups like Run DMC, the Beastie Boys, and KRS-One. He fell in love with the deep beats, the funky rhythms, and the fast lyrics, which he could easily relate to.

After doing his homework and playing with his friends, Sean would spend much of his time watching videos on music television programs, hoping to catch his favorite rap artists. Sometimes, he would even sneak out of bed when he wasn't sleepy and stay up until the wee hours of the morning watching the music videos. Sean would mimic the music and the raps. He pictured himself performing the songs. He would always sneak back in bed before his mother found out.

Janice may have been too tired to notice that her son was secretly getting up to listen to music. She held down three jobs—bus driver, assistant teacher, and salesclerk at a clothing shop—to give her family a good life. She saved enough money and worked hard enough to be able to put Sean in private school.

Sean realized from an early age that he needed to start helping out around the house, and by the time he was twelve years old he landed his first job. He became a newspaper delivery boy.

Sean realized from an early age that he needed to start helping out around the house, and by the time he was twelve . . . he landed his first job.

"Like a lot of kids who grow up in single parent homes, I had to get a job much quicker and start thinking about the future much earlier," Sean said. "I had to help out and become the man of the house sooner."

He even had to lie about his age to get the job, and then he talked a friend into getting a job as well so that Sean could do both routes. This was just an example of how hard Sean was willing to work to get the things he wanted. He obviously took his cue from his mother, who was probably the hardest worker that Sean ever saw.

> ***When Sean turned fourteen, Janice was earning enough money to send him to Mount St. Michael Academy in the Bronx.***

That hard work paid off. When Sean turned fourteen, Janice was earning enough money to send him to Mount St. Michael Academy in the Bronx. This was a Catholic high school known for its tough discipline and good teachers. Sean would have a better chance getting into a decent college if he did well at the Mount, as it was called.

During high school, Sean became exposed to even more cultures. He also got a chance to hear a lot of rock music during that time, listening to his friends' tapes of Black Sabbath and Led Zeppelin. He listened to the music with an open mind, but it was clear his passion was still rap. He was a slave to the sound.

Sean worked two and sometimes three jobs after school. He even worked at an amusement park, where some of his classmates would tease him. It didn't matter to him. He wanted to be able to have money to buy the music he liked to listen to and the clothes that he wanted to wear.

Somehow, the music gave Sean confidence. Hearing it, he felt that he was hip, that he was cool. He soon started going down to Harlem to hang out with his old friends and listen to rap and hip-hop sounds.

That's when he started answering to the name Puffy. It would be the first of many nicknames for the young teenager who had his sights set on making history.

"I would always say to myself that I wanted to be somebody who makes history," he said.

Kids are very important to P. Diddy, who donates a lot of his money to fund children's programs.

From College Student to Businessman

Listening to music with his friends not only made Sean, or Puffy, confident around people, but it also helped make him a great dancer. He and his friends would go to all the big dance and rap clubs in New York City, and soon Puffy was making a name for himself as a dancer. After a while he wouldn't even have to wait in line. The owners of the clubs would drag him inside so that he could excite the crowds.

Puffy started making the right connections on the dance floor. Record executives and performers noticed him. By the time he graduated from high school, the skinny kid that somehow also played on the high school football team had appeared in several music videos, including some by the Fine Young Cannibals, Doug E. Fresh, and Babyface.

Sean did not let his mother down, however. After high school he chose to attend Howard University, a predominantly black college located in the Washington, D.C., area. He didn't know this then, but by the time he arrived on campus, Sean was already a semi-celebrity. People knew who he was from his work in music videos. He was the big man on campus.

After a few months, Puffy and a friend decided they could make money and the right contacts by hosting great dance parties at the school. Puffy was able to talk certain celebrities and rap entertainers to come and hang out. The parties became the hit of the college, and Sean was meeting all types of people that could possibly help him in the music industry.

For the first time in his life, Sean "Puffy" Combs thought that he could actually turn his love of music and rap into a career.

For the first time in his life, Sean "Puffy" Combs thought that he could actually turn his love of music and rap into a career.

It wouldn't take long. One of his friends was successful rapper Heavy D. Sean asked Heavy D to help him get an internship at Uptown Records. Uptown was a label that catered mainly to the rap and hip-hop crowd.

Puffy worked as hard as he ever had before. He took notes about everything. He soon had notebooks filled with what everybody does at a record company. Puffy found himself working eighty hours a week and going to school at the same time. It was an impossible schedule. He dropped out of school, explaining to his angry mother that this was his big chance.

Puffy found himself working eighty hours a week and going to school at the same time. It was an impossible schedule.

Puffy had a knack for knowing what the people wanted. Single-handedly, he transformed the image of singer Jodeci to one that was not so glitzy and more urban friendly. Jodeci became a big hit. In 1992 Puffy was promoted to vice president of the record company.

One of the first really big things Puffy did was sign a 350-pound rapper by the name of Biggie, also known as the Notorious B.I.G., to the label. Things didn't work out with Uptown Records, however, and Puffy started his own record company: Bad Boy.

It was there that he and Biggie perfected that East Coast Sound. Puffy appeared on several of Biggie's songs, lending his own newly developing rap voice to the tapes. They were a hit. But soon a rivalry erupted

The crowd goes wild when P. Diddy takes the stage with his friends Busta Rhymes, Pharrell Williams, and Usher.

between East Coast and West Coast Rap. Insults began to fly back and forth. Rappers threatened each other in their music.

In 1996, West Coast rapper Tupac Shakur was murdered. Six months later, so was Puffy's friend, the Notorious B.I.G. He was gunned down just as his last recordings would rise to the top of the music charts and propel him into stardom.

Puffy was shattered by the killings. He wanted to do something special to honor his friend. He was inspired by an old rock ballad by a group named The Police called "Every Breath You Take."

What he decided to do would change his life forever. It would also change the landscape of rap and popular music.

Family is the most important thing to P. Diddy. He loves spending time with his children and taking them on vacation with him.

Rap Superstar and Beyond

Sean "Puffy" Combs wrote lyrics about his slain best friend and recorded the song over samples of the old Police song. He called the piece "I'll Be Missing You." It became the biggest song of 1997, and Puffy recorded an album to go along with the tribute.

Titled *Can't Nobody Hold Me Down*, the album sold more than seven million copies and held the top spot on the music charts for more than two months. Suddenly, and perhaps quite by accident, this record company executive was now a rap superstar. The album had six hit singles and earned Sean two Grammy Awards—the industry's highest award.

He sang his tribute for his friend at the 1998 MTV Video Music Awards, and he brought the house down. Rap had been popular for many years, but this seemed to be the moment that it was accepted in mainstream households throughout America.

Seeing that his record appealed to both white and black audiences, and seeing that it appealed to those who liked rap as well as those who liked rock, Sean decided to continue to try to bring those two different worlds together.

After one album Puffy had become a music pioneer. He had become an expert at how to pick just the right sound . . . to use as background for his raps.

He collaborated on songs with rock groups like the Foo Fighters and with legendary rocker Jimmy Page. These songs helped inspire a whole new type of rap/rock that would later be made famous by people like Kid Rock and Limp Bizkit. After one album Puffy had become a music pioneer. He had become an expert at how to pick just the right sound, whether it was an old hit song or a new groove, to use as background for his raps. He also knew how much sampling from a record would give a new recording a fresh new sound. The fans ate it up!

In 1999, he released his second album, *Forever*, which also became an instant hit. During this time Puffy's love life also made the headlines. He was dating one of his protégés, Jennifer Lopez. The two made all the gossip columns but eventually broke up in 2001.

Sean Combs changed his nickname from Puffy to P. Diddy and decided to go outside the music industry and try other things. Like any successful businessman, P. Diddy knew it would be smart to have a lot of different options. In 1998 he started a clothing line called Sean John Clothing. The clothes at first were meant to appeal to the urban male, but as critics hailed the clothing line, the appeal expanded.

In 2000, Sean was nominated for the Perry Ellis Award for Best Menswear Designer of the Year by the Council of Fashion Designers of America. Soon after, he launched a clothing line for boys and then in 2002 for women. Unlike traditional rap-style clothing, Sean John clothes can be found all over mainstream America. They are sold in chain department stores such as Macy's and Bloomingdale's. In 2004, the Perry Ellis Award for Best Menswear Designer was his.

P. Diddy also started acting. He appeared in a few movies and then on Broadway in *A Raisin in the Sun*. He also opened up a restaurant in New York City.

Even though he has started to branch out and explore other things, fans of that special P. Diddy sound

P. Diddy started his own hip, urban clothing line calling it "Sean John."

will not be disappointed. The record producer, songwriter, and rapper shows no signs of slowing down.

Bad Boy Records continues to produce music, and rapper P. Diddy will certainly lend his suave and sophisticated sound to the records.

P. Diddy is also one to remember where he came from. In 1995 he founded Daddy's House Social Programs, Inc. His organization tutors hundreds of inner-city kids on their schoolwork every weekend during the school year. It also teaches people about finances and the stock market, takes high school seniors on tours of college campuses, and gives outstanding students the chance to travel to other countries. Every summer, Daddy's House Sleep Away Camps sends about 200 New York City kids to campgrounds in upstate New York.

In 2003 he decided to run in the famous New York City Marathon as a way of raising money to help the children of New York. Did he ever! P. Diddy finished the marathon in four hours and fourteen minutes and raised two million dollars. The money went to New York City Public Schools, The Children's Hope Foundation, and Daddy's House Social Programs.

He also promises to stick close to his roots. He has a home in Manhattan, where he raises his two sons, Justin and Christian, and his stepson, Quincy.

"I'm a definite stereotypical New Yorker," Combs said. "I love the Yankees, the Mets—I love everything about New York."

When P. Diddy is performing on stage, he feels the most at home.

1970 Sean Combs is born November 4.

1973 His father is killed in a drug deal.

1990 Sean "Puffy" Combs is named vice president of Uptown Records.

1993 Puffy starts Bad Boy Entertainment.

1994 Son, Justin Combs, is born.

1995 Puffy branches out, producing artists like Aretha Franklin and Mariah Carey. He establishes Daddy's House Social Programs, Inc.

1997 Notorious B.I.G. is shot and killed. Puffy releases his first album, which includes the hit song "I'll be Missing You." Son, Christian Casey Combs, is born.

1998 Puffy wins two Grammy Awards. He starts Sean John Clothing line.

2001 Now P. Diddy, he appears in the films *Made* and *Monster's Ball.*

2003 Runs in New York City Marathon to raise money for charity.

2004 P. Diddy wins third Grammy Award with Nelly and Murphy Lee. He stars on Broadway in *A Raisin in the Sun.* He wins the Perry Ellis Award for Best Menswear Designer of the Year.

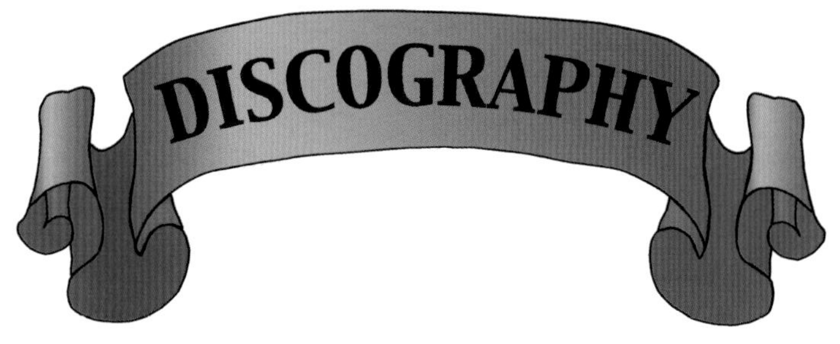

Albums

2004 *PD5*
2002 *P. Diddy and Bad Boys: We Invented the Remix Vol. 1*
2001 *The Saga Continues*
1999 *Forever*
1997 *No Way Out*

Hit Singles

2004 "Breathe, Stretch, Shake" (Mase with P. Diddy)
"I Don't Wanna Know" (Mario Winans with Enya & P. Diddy)
2003 "Shake Ya Tailfeather" (P. Diddy, Nelly & Murphy Lee)
"Bump, Bump, Bump" (B2K & Puff Daddy)
2002 "I Need A Girl (Part One)" (with Usher & Loon)
"I Need A Girl (Part Two)" (P. Diddy and Ginuwine with Loon, Mario Winans & Tammy Ruggeri)
2001 "Bad Boy for Life" (P. Diddy, Black Rob & Marc Curry)
1999 "All Night Long" (Faith Evans with Puff Daddy)
"Satisfy You" (with R. Kelly)
1998 "Come With Me" (with Jimmy Page)
"Lookin' at Me" (with Mase)
"Been Around the World"
"It's All About the Benjamins"
"Victory" (Puff Daddy & The Family/The Notorious B.I.G./Busta Rhymes)
1997 "Mo Money Mo Problems" (The Notorious B.I.G. with Mase and Puff Daddy)
"Can't Nobody Hold Me Down" (with Mase)
"I'll Be Missing You" (with Faith Evans and 112)
"Someone" (SWV with Puff Daddy)

Sound Track Contributions

2002 *The Wild Thornberrys Movie*
All About the Benjamins

Acting Credits
Movies
2001 *Made*
Monster's Ball

Broadway Plays
2004 *A Raisin in the Sun*

Awards and Nominations
1997 Billboard Music Award for Top Rap Artist
Billboard Music Award for Top Rap Album
1998 Grammy Award for Best Rap Performance by a Duo or Group for "I'll Be Missing You" (with Faith Evans and 112)
Grammy Award for Best Rap Album, *No Way Out*
1999 Blockbuster Entertainment Award nomination for Favorite Song from a Movie, "Come With Me" from *Godzilla*
2004 Grammy Award for Best Rap Performance by a Duo or Group (with Nelly and Murphy Lee)
Perry Ellis Award for Best Menswear Designer of the Year

INDEX